D0409391

FIND OUT ABOUT

ANCIENT EGYPT

STEWART ROSS

HODDER
Wayland

an imprint of Hodder Children's Books

First published in 2006 by Hodder Wayland,
an imprint of Hodder Children's Books

© Hodder Wayland 2006

Project Editor: Kirsty Hamilton
Designer: Simon Borrough
Maps: Peter Bull

British Library Cataloguing in Publication Data
Ross, Stewart
Find out about ancient Egypt
1. Egypt - Civilization - To 332 B.C. - Juvenile literature
2. Egypt - History - To 332 B.C. - Juvenile literature
3. Egypt - Antiquities - Juvenile literature
I. Title II.Ancient Egypt
932

ISBN 07502 45956

Colour Reproduction by Dot Gradations Ltd, UK
Printed in China

Hodder Children's Books
A division of Hodder Headline Limited
338 Euston Road, London NW1 3BH

The publisher would like to thank the following for permission to
reproduce their pictures: Title page, 22 (bottom), 23, 25, 26, 28, 31, 35,
45(bottom), Gianni Dagli Orti / Corbis; 3, 27, 30, Francis G.Mayer /
Corbis; 5, Digital Image © 1996 Corbis / original image courtesy of NASA
/ Corbis; 6 Charles & Josette Lenars / Corbis; 7, Richard T. Nowitz /
Coribs; 8, Paul Almasy / Corbis; 9, Roger Ressmeyer / Corbis; 11, 43, Roger
Wood / Corbis; 12, Carmen Redondo / Corbis; 13 (top), Dave Bartruff /
Corbis; 13 (bottom) Adam Woolfitt / Corbis; 14, akg images / Andrea
Jemolo; 15, Werner Forman / Corbis; 16, akg-images / Erich Lessing; 18,
North Carolina Museum of Art / Corbis; 19, Stapleton Collection / Corbis;
20, Werner Forman Archive/ E. Strouhal; 21, Werner Forman Archive /
British Museum no.32610; 22 (top), 24, 29, 33, 34, 36, 41, Archivo
Incongrafico, S.A / Corbis; 32, 37, SandroVannini / Corbis; 38, 45(top),
Bettman / Corbis; 39, akg images / Robert O'Dea; 40, akg-images / Erich
Lessing; 44, Historical Picture Archive / Corbis

CONTENTS

WHO WERE THE ANCIENT EGYPTIANS?

Egypt was home to the longest-lived and most startling of all ancient civilizations. Its achievements, especially in art, government and construction, made Egypt one of the ancient world's most advanced civilizations. Remarkably, though, all this was done in a most unfavourable environment.

Egypt is a large, mostly barren land in north-east Africa. It is bordered on two sides by sea, the Mediterranean to the north and the Red Sea to the east. To the south is Sudan and, further off, the uplands of Central Africa. The western frontier is mostly desert. What binds Egypt together, what makes its geography distinctive, is the mighty River Nile that flows the length of the country before emptying itself into the Mediterranean.

It was to the green areas on either bank of this river that Stone Age settlers came, around 5000 BC, and set up farming communities. The land was less arid than today, and the communities thrived and expanded into one of the world's great civilizations.

The people of ancient Egypt were not a racially distinct group: the Arabs that make up the bulk of modern Egypt were in ancient times mostly confined to the Arabian

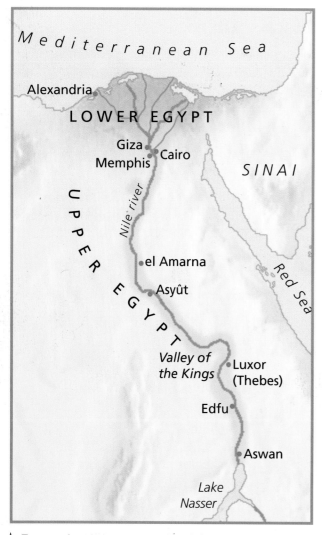

▲ Egypt, showing geographical features, modern towns and ancient sites.

▲ A view of the delta of the River Nile (the dark triangle at the bottom), seen from outer space in 2003.

peninsular. The citizens of ancient Egypt were a mix of African, Mediterranean and European peoples. They thought of themselves as a distinct civilization because of how they lived, not because of their appearance. Members of several racial groups could be found at all levels of society.

THE NILE

Ancient Egyptian civilization centered around the River Nile. Without the river there would have been no civilization – it was, literally, the Egyptians' river of life.

Before the building of the Aswan Dam in the later 20th century, once a year rainwater from mountains far to the south poured into the river and caused it to flood along most of its length. This flooding deposited rich silt (soil) along the banks. The flood (or 'inundation', around July-September) was one of Egypt's three seasons. The other two were the growing season after the waters had subsided (roughly October-April) and the dry season (May-June).

The inundation was the most important season of the year. By leaving fresh layers of new soil along the Nile's banks, it allowed the Egyptians to grow crops that

would not otherwise have survived in the dusty desert. Without the corn grown along the fertile strip beside the river, settled life for large numbers of people would have been impossible. More than sufficient food was grown, so some was exported. Moreover, the easy farming conditions gave workers spare time in which to work on other projects.

⊲ An ancient Egyptian fresco of a wife watching her husband ploughing fields with oxen.

Ancient water-meter

WHAT DOES IT TELL US?

Although this looks like a set of steps, it is in fact a Nilometer – a means of measuring the height of the River Nile. The height of the inundation (shown by the height of the water on the central column) was of great importance in ancient Egypt. Some scholars have suggested that taxes (in the form of produce) depended on the height of the water: high flood = more land irrigated = more tax!

WHAT DOES IT TELL US?

More than 7,000 years ago people settled in communities along the fertile banks of the River Nile. About 2,000 years later these communities were united into the state of Egypt under a single king. For the next 3,000 years Egypt was one of the richest, most cultured and best ordered states in the world. Impressive evidence of its past greatness survives in the form of mighty pyramids and temples. Ancient Egyptian power declined in the first millennium BCE until, in 30 BCE, it was absorbed into the Roman Empire.

The importance of the inundation in ancient Egyptian life is emphasised by the focus on Hapy, the god of the inundation. He is basically a male figure with a pot-belly. However, he also has large breasts and a head-dress of plants. His physical attributes make him a fitting symbol of the fertility provided by the swelling river.

As well as allowing irrigation for agriculture, the Nile had numerous other functions. It was almost the only source of drinking water for people and beasts. Numerous fish were caught in it, too. Its reedy banks were home to the birds that Egyptians hunted for food. The reeds themselves were cut, dried and used for a wide variety of purposes. Finally, the water of the Nile was Egypt's main highway.

A GREAT CIVILIZATION

Other striking aspects of ancient Egyptian civilization include its duration, the power of its leaders, and its majestic

⋏ A sunk relief sculpture of two images of the Nile-god Hapy, tying together Upper and Lower Egypt.

monuments. Most impressive is the sheer length of time over which it survived – 3,000 years (c. 3100-30 BCE). Some idea of the scale of this is evident if we compare it with the duration of the ancient Roman civilization which was a mere 800 years.

Another interesting characteristic of ancient Egypt is the position held by its kings and queens. Rarely have human beings had such power. The king did not just rule the land. He was also feared and even sometimes worshipped as a god. Egyptian royal women had more power and influence than women in other early civilizations.

The parts of ancient Egypt that most people know best are its towering monuments, in particular the Sphinx and the Great Pyramid of Giza. These are the most impressive pieces of evidence of the Egyptians' brilliant skills as builders and organisers. The pyramids were royal burial sites in which everything a monarch might need in the afterlife was buried with them. Because they were essentially religious monuments, they are a vivid reminder of the central part that religion played in Egyptians' lives.

The most magnificent evidence of all

WHAT DOES IT TELL US?

The Great Pyramid of Giza (right), one of the wonders of the world, was built some 4,500 years ago. It is a mine of information about ancient Egypt. Precisely constructed from 3.2 million blocks of limestone weighing an average 2.5 tonnes each, it leaves us staggered by the skills and organisation of the people who carved out these blocks so accurately, moved them to the building site and fitted them together so precisely. Its function as a royal burial chamber, pointing to the sky, is strong evidence of the importance and power of the king who ordered it to be built (Khufu, 2589-2566 BCE), and the primary importance of religion in ancient Egyptian culture. The pyramids of Menkaure (left) and Khafre (centre) are also shown below.

HOW WERE THE ANCIENT EGYPTIANS RULED?

For thousands of years Egypt was one of the most efficiently ruled states in the world. At the heart of its government was the king or, occasionally, queen. Known in later times by the even grander title of 'pharaoh' (see page 11), ancient Egyptian monarchs were considered more than just rulers. They were seen as god-like, living symbols of Egypt itself.

TWO BECOMES ONE

Egypt's civilization first flourished along the banks of the River Nile in southern (Upper) and northern (Lower) Egypt. These areas were occupied by various tribes, each with its own chief. Gradually, the many tribes came under a single leader for the north and another for the south. These leaders were perhaps the world's first kings.

Around 3100 BCE, the king of Upper Egypt conquered the South and became ruler of the whole country. Tradition says his name was 'Menes'. Scholars reckon this is myth and say the true first king of all Egypt was not Menes but either King Narmer or King Aha.

THE DYNASTIES

King Aha was the first king of the first 'dynasty' or ruling family. This dynasty provided eight kings. It was followed by the second dynasty, with seven kings, and so on to the thirtieth dynasty almost three millennia later.

Dynasties did not always follow smoothly on from each other. Occasionally there were rebellions and civil wars, when government came close to collapse. These years are called 'Intermediate Periods'. Ancient Egypt suffered three of them: the First Intermediate Period (2181-2055 BCE), the Second Intermediate Period (1650-1550 BCE) and the Third Intermediate Period (1069-747 BCE).

Between the Intermediate Periods were three periods known as 'Kingdoms': the Old Kingdom (2686-2181 BCE), the Middle Kingdom (2055-1650 BCE) and the New Kingdom (1550-1069 BCE). Each had its dynasties and distinct cultural style. The country's most famous monuments, the Great Pyramid and the Sphinx, date from the Old Kingdom. We are best informed about the New Kingdom because it was the most recent and there is more evidence in existence from this period. It also provided some of Egypt's most famous monarchs, such as Rameses II the Great (1279-1213 BCE).

⋏ A detail from the painted casket of Tutankhamun. King Tutankhamun (c. 1370-1352 BCE) is shown scattering his enemies.

KING-GODS

Religion and ruling could not be separated in ancient Egypt. The king's job was to preserve harmony (*Maat*) on Earth, and since this harmony was thought to be god-given the king needed god-like powers. Thus, from the earliest times, the king was regarded as part-god.

Some of the early kings were thought of as actual gods, masters of the universe. After about 2180 BCE, the king's divine status on Earth became less certain. Nevertheless, there was no doubt that after death they became gods. Their earthly title of 'pharaoh', in use by the New Kingdom, originally meant simply 'great house' (*per aa*) or royal palace. Over time it came to mean the most important person from that palace – the king himself.

From an Egyptian account of the Battle of Qadesh:

'His majesty ... arrayed himself in [put on] his coat of mail. He ... charged into the foes of the vanquished chief ... and the numerous countries which were with him. His majesty was ... great in strength, smiting and slaying among them; his majesty hurled them headlong, one upon another.'

WHAT DOES IT TELL US?

At first glance this quotation suggests that the king, Rameses II, was a brave warrior. Other evidence, however, indicates that the writer exaggerates Rameses' valour. The piece may be more valuable for showing how kings may have been flattered by their people than for giving factual information.

Each king had five names, each of them reinforcing his status. His second name was always his 'Horus' name, linking him to the falcon-god Horus, the protector of kingship. As the falcon flew high above the land, so the king was thought to soar over Egypt. Another mark of a king's importance is found in the system of dates. This did not link one reign to another; instead, dates started with the first year of each king's reign, as if time itself began with each new ruler.

ALL-POWERFUL

The king was principal administrator, chief priest and army commander, although in practice he usually handed down these functions to ministers, priests and generals. Marriage customs were another sign of the king's remarkable status. Because of his god-like position the king was not bound by normal earthly rules. His many wives, for example, could include his own sisters and daughters. The powerful Queen Hatshepsut, for instance, was one of the wives of her brother, Thutmose II.

In theory the Double Crown of Upper and Lower Egypt, worn by kings after the unification of the country, passed down from father to son. In practice things were not so simple. Some kings (such as Apepi II) were unimpressive; others probably devoted themselves more to personal pleasure than the tasks of government. As a result of the activities

Royal glory in ruins

WHAT DOES IT TELL US?

Rameses III emerged before his people in this raised 'window of appearances' in the temple-palace at Medinet Habu below. The height shows how he wished to be seen literally above his subjects. His physical supremacy represented his semi-divine status. Also, the window faces east, towards the rising sun, so the king would appear with the sun shining upon him.

of incompetent rulers, Egyptian history is littered with stories of plot and rebellion. This allowed men like the talented Horemeb to climb from nothing to the highest position in the land. He joined the army, rose to become its

⋏ The remains of the Mortuary Temple of Queen Hatshepsut at Luxor, Egypt.

commander during the reign of Tutankhamun, and was eventually declared king in 1323 BCE.

Royal women always had power either as the king's mother, his chief wife or one of his other wives. Some, such as Queen Nefertiti, became as powerful as the king himself. The most remarkable was Hatshepsut (1473-1458 BCE), who ruled as queen and king (and was called pharaoh) while Thutmose III (c. 1479-1425 BCE) was still a child. She is shown wearing the royal false beard and inscriptions refer to her as 'he'!

Two crowns, one king

WHAT DOES IT TELL US?

This sculpture shows the Double Crown of Upper and Lower Egypt. It reminds us that the king was known as 'Lord of the Two Lands' and that Egypt had once been two kingdoms. The first kings are shown wearing just the white crown of Upper Egypt. When combined with the red crown of Lower Egypt it produced the 'Two Mighty Ones'. The Double Crown shows how keen kings were to emphasise Egypt's unity.

ADMINISTRATION

The leading officials beneath a king were his vizier (a sort of prime minister), his chief priests and his buildings managers. At the time of a king like Rameses II (the Great), who built an enormous number of monuments, the buildings' managers were second only to the king in importance. Also powerful were the military commanders. Thutmose III, a formidable soldier, took personal command of his armies, while Seti I (1294-1279 BCE) relied on his vizier Amenemope to lead a successful campaign against the Nubians to the south.

At court the vizier (of whom there were sometimes more than one) was assisted by a treasurer, chief steward and other household officials. Royal power extended over the rest of the country through both a system of religious organisation, run through the temples,

⋀ A wall painting (c.1400-1390 BCE) showing two 'rope-stretchers' marking out the boundaries of a field.

and another system for keeping law and order and seeing that taxes were paid. Under the second system the kingdom was divided between Upper and Lower Egypt, then each part was further split up into districts called *nomes*.

A *nome* was looked after by an official called a *nomarch*. A *nomarch* was served by scribes who checked accounts, collected tax (usually in the form of corn), oversaw the law and made sure fields were the correct size. Scribes called 'rope-stretchers' marked out boundaries: because the inundation washed away boundaries each year, fields had to be re-marked every autumn by using ropes as if they were tape-measures.

HOW DID EGYPT GET ALONG WITH ITS NEIGHBOURS?

The Egyptians believed they were superior to all other people on earth. It is not difficult to see why: they knew nothing of great civilizations elsewhere in the world, such as China, and their wealth, organisation and skills certainly made them appear more able than their neighbours. This feeling of superiority did not stop the Egyptians from having contact with those living beyond their borders but not all of it was pleasant.

TRADE AND TRIBUTE

Two aspects of the Egyptians' way of life made trade difficult: they did not use money until late in the first millennium BCE, and in theory the state (the king) owned everything. Consequently, it is rare to hear of Egyptian traders or merchants operating on their own.

One of the country's best-known trading missions was that which Queen Hatshepsut (see page 13) sent down the

Egypt meets the wider world

WHAT DOES IT TELL US?

This scene is carved on the walls of Hatshepsut's temple at Deir el-Bahri. It shows Egyptian traders in the land of Punt. They are laying out their goods while the people of Punt lay out theirs. The carving is excellent evidence for the type of goods traded and for the fact that trade was done by barter rather than by purchase (money).

Red Sea to the land of 'Punt' (somewhere on the coast of East Africa). The Egyptian ships took cloth, grain, papyrus, copper and gems. They bartered (swapped) these for exotic products like myrrh (including whole myrrh trees), gold, ebony, ivory, wild animals (including baboons who were sacred to the Egyptians) and slaves.

To the north the Egyptians exchanged goods with the lands of the Eastern Mediterranean, while caravans of mules and donkeys carried merchandise back and forth across the desert to the west. As with the African trade, Egypt's main products of exchange were grain and cloth. They imported timber, spices and some metals. Most goods were carried in foreign boats from ports such as Byblos in Lebanon, although by the time of the New Kingdom some Egyptian temples had fleets of their own to trade with.

Goods were traded in the monarch's name. Materials entering Egypt were labelled as 'tribute' (offerings) from lesser peoples to the Great King. Goods going the other way were described as gifts to people 'beyond respect'. No foreign nation was admitted to have a king – he was called simply 'chief' or 'big man'. The Egyptians claimed that only they had a true king.

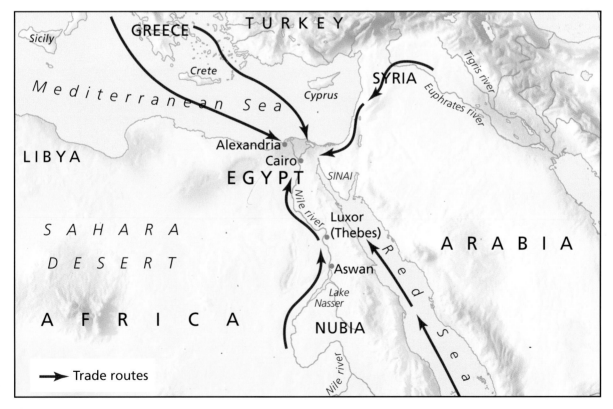

Ʌ Major trade routes used by the ancient Egyptians. (Some locations are identified by their present names.)

WAR AND NUBIA

Wealthy Egypt was a tempting target for attackers. Its survival for 3,000 years shows its military as well as economic strength. By the time of the New Kingdom it had a well-organised, permanent army of chariots and foot soldiers for defending and expanding the frontiers. Favoured weapons appear to have been spears. The infantry also carried leather shields and the higher-ranking soldiers had body armour.

The most troublesome frontier was with Nubia, the land to the south where the Nile makes a huge 'S' bend. For many hundreds of years the Nubians raided Egypt in search of precious loot, while the Egyptians tried to conquer Nubia for its valuable gold, slaves and exotic African products such as incense.

Eventually, during the New Kingdom, the Egyptians overcame Nubia and built stout fortresses there to maintain control.

EMPIRE

Until around 1800 BCE attacks on Egypt from the Mediterranean and across the Sinai Peninsula had been largely in the form of raids. However, during the Second Intermediate Period (see page 10) the Hyksos people from Syria-Palestine came to rule large parts of Egypt. The Egyptians regained this land during the

Ⅴ A model of a Nile boat from the Middle Kingdom.

WHAT DOES IT TELL US?

This copy of an ancient Egyptian painting shows Rameses II galloping towards his enemies in a chariot. It gives the impression that he is triumphing over them without difficulty. Most kings, whether successful warriors or not, were shown in this way. The picture is designed to build up a powerful image of Rameses rather than record an historical event.

New Kingdom when they went on the attack and carved out an empire along the eastern seaboard of the Mediterranean. At its largest, under Thutmose I (1493-1482 BCE), the empire reached from the River Euphrates in the north to Kurgus in the south. It had also expanded west into Libya. The benefits of empire were enormous. Into Egypt poured vast quantities of tribute in the form of gold, silver, timber, spices, scents and other commodities. The Egyptians had never known such wealth.

The survival of the empire depended on the ability of its rulers. By the time of Rameses III (1184-1153 BCE) the Egyptian Empire was already in decline and 'Sea People' from the Aegean area were threatening the homeland. Egyptian power collapsed further under Rameses' successors until the country divided and fell to successive invaders.

Rameses III records how he prepares for an attack of the Sea People. From an inscription found at the temple-palace of Medinet Habu:

'I … prepared the river mouth like a strong wall with warships, galleys, and skiffs. They were completely equipped both fore and aft with brave fighters carrying their weapons and infantry of all the pick of Egypt, being like roaring lions upon the mountain.'

WHAT DOES IT TELL US?

This extract suggests many things. First, Rameses III clearly knew that the Sea People were coming and was therefore able to get his defences ready. Second, at that time Egypt had a navy, or at least sea-going ships that the king could use in time of war. Third, naval warfare seems to have been fought by ships carrying soldiers, like a land battle at sea.

WHAT WAS LIFE LIKE IN ANCIENT EGYPT?

It is not easy to imagine what everyday life was like in ancient Egypt. The Egyptians did not know about many things – electricity, for instance – that we take for granted. Nor did they have much idea of civilizations elsewhere. By our standards, most Egyptians lived short, tough and ignorant lives.

That said, certain pieces of evidence, such as a statue of a loving couple, remind us that we are basically the same as our distant Egyptian ancestors. Like us, they laughed and cried, fell in love, lived in families and gazed in wonder at the sky. Thus, although their daily lives were very different from ours, their basic needs, instincts and emotions were similar.

Evidence under the desert

WHAT DOES IT TELL US?

These are the remains of a village for workers digging royal graves in the Valley of the Kings. The site offers valuable information about the size, shape, and construction of houses. The density of the housing and the narrowness of the streets suggests that the community was probably well organised to manage matters like water and sewage. Unfortunately, we cannot tell how typical this village was.

WHAT DOES IT TELL US?

This limestone carving of a house, dating from the Third Intermediate Period (1070-747 BCE), is a valuable source of information on Egyptian domestic life. The small door and tiny, barred windows are probably like that for security reasons, which suggests that burglary was not uncommon. Notice the flat roof above the ground floor, edged with a parapet. As there seems to be no inside access, there was probably a stairway up the outside of the house.

AT HOME

The royal family lived in grand palaces. Archaeological evidence suggests that these were huge buildings with many rooms to accommodate the king's family, courtiers, servants and slaves. The public rooms were decorated with tiles and paintings. At the heart of the palace, in a hall of many pillars, the king's throne stood on a raised platform. Wealthy families lived in spacious villas with enclosed gardens and pools of cooling water. Like the palaces, the interior walls were brightly painted and the floors laid with coloured tiles.

Little is known about the homes of ordinary people. The Egyptians thought they were not worth describing in words or pictures, and over the millennia they have either been pulled down or have largely crumbled away. From models, and remaining foundations and lower parts of the walls, it seems that ordinary houses were made of mud brick. The windows were tiny and there were normally no more than four rooms at ground level. It is assumed that they used the roof for storage and sleeping in hot weather.

The interior of most houses must have been dark and bleak, with little decoration or furniture. Excavated ruins show us that there were often brick benches around the walls, some wooden three-legged stools, and a low table. Pegs on the walls and baskets woven from reeds provided storage. Cooking was probably done outside on an open fire.

Nebamun hunting

WHAT DOES IT TELL US?

This picture, painted on the tomb of the scribe Nebamun, shows him hunting with a throwing stick. His wife, at the rear of the boat, and his daughter, holding her father's leg, look on. The family cat goes into the reeds after the birds his master has hit. The painting is excellent evidence on hunting practices, the types of birds caught, for instance, ducks, and even dress and jewellery (although Nebamun's wife seems a bit over-dressed for a hunting trip).

AT TABLE

The basic diet of most Egyptians was bread, vegetables and fruit. They made their bread from barley or a grain known as emmer wheat. They also made cakes and pastries from these grains, and used barley for brewing beer. They baked bread on the outside surface of tall, pottery ovens in which fires burned. The loaves

➤ A relief carving of a man fishing with a net, in the marshes of the River Nile.

were flat, round and rather tough. Common vegetables were beans, lentils, leeks, onions and lettuces. Melons, figs and dates grew on the river bank and in orchards irrigated by its waters. Pomegranates were a special luxury reserved for the wealthy or for feast days. Herbs and spices livened up dull meals, while cooking oil was crushed from plants such as flax. Milk and cheese were not plentiful.

The Nile provided fresh fish, especially perch, and those living on the coast had an even wider variety of catch. Poorer families did not eat meat regularly. Many kept goats (which also gave them milk, cheese and wool) and geese for eggs. Some temples owned a herd of cattle, which were valuable animals; sheep and pigs were also quite rare. This meant beef, mutton and pork were luxuries. More common was meat got by hunting the ducks and geese that lived in the thick Nile marshes.

Bread, fish, vegetables, fruit ... the diet of the average Egyptian was certainly very healthy. None of their food was processed and the fat content was very low. Most of it was fresh, too, because the Egyptians could preserve it only by drying it in the sun, pickling it, smoking or salting it. The dry climate meant that grain could be stored without going rotten, although rodents and insects were a constant problem.

Edible evidence

WHAT DOES IT TELL US?

This Egyptian wall painting of servants bringing food for a feast gives a fair idea of the range of food eaten at the time. As well as fruits (including grapes and pomegranates) there are huge fish, marrows, ducks and geese. The man at the top has a string of small fish that, because they are to be served at a feast, may have been a delicacy. Note how all the food is fresh and makes up a well-balanced diet.

PARTY TIME

The Egyptians liked a good party! Feasts were always religious, either to thank a deity for a personal benefit, such as the birth of a healthy child, or as part of a public festival. For a feast the guests dressed in their best clothes and jewels, and applied their make-up with care. Entertainment was provided by speakers and singers, musicians and dancers, jugglers and jesters.

Beer was the most widely drunk alcoholic beverage. Egyptians made beer by fermenting barley and barley loaves.

They were also wine experts. They made their wine from several grape varieties and stored it in labelled jars like modern-

Party time!

WHAT DOES IT TELL US?

This picture, painted on the wall of a tomb at Thebes, gives us details of dancing girls, a pipe player, women's dress, braided hair and jewellery. More mysterious are the strange objects on the ladies' heads. It used to be thought that these were cones of scented wax that released perfume as they melted. Scholars now suggest that they are just representative of goodness, like haloes in Christian pictures.

ʌ An Egyptian wall painting showing men harvesting grapes for wine-making.

day wine bottles. As well as home-made wine, those who could afford to drank rich wines imported from the lands of the eastern Mediterranean, such as Lebanon.

Festivals took place around the Nile. In the Opet Festival the statue of Amun was hauled upstream from Karnak to Luxor in a mysterious ritual that reconfirmed royal power. The Festival of the Beautiful Embrace celebrated the union of Horus and Hathor. The festival took the form of a marriage between the two deities. The statue of Hathor was taken to meet the statue of Horus where the 'beautiful embrace' (the details are not known) took place.

Extract from the story of the deities Isis and Osiris:

'In celebration, Seth … held a spectacular feast at his city of Tanis … Tales were told, boasts exchanged, dances performed, and much beer was consumed.'

WHAT DOES IT TELL US?

Because Egyptian gods and goddesses were believed to have human characteristics, the writer gives his story a human setting. The piece suggests many things about the customs at Egyptian feasts. It reveals for instance, that beer was drunk, and that dancing was an entertainment. Furthermore, it seems evident that the guests enjoyed story-telling and exaggerated conversation.

ʌ A wall painting (c.1400-1390 BCE) of elegant ladies at a concert.

GETTING DRESSED

During the 3,000 years of Egyptian civilization, clothing styles remained surprisingly similar. Everyday wear for ordinary people hardly changed at all. Working men wore a loin cloth made of linen or leather, and women wore a straight-sided sheath dress with straps across the shoulder. Nakedness was not frowned upon amongst the children and slaves were often shown wearing no clothes at all.

Formal menswear consisted of a kind of kilt, which by the New Kingdom was pleated. By the first millennium BCE it had become baggier still. There is also evidence of men wearing linen shirts.

Women's dresses evolved from two shoulder straps to one. Later, Greek designs became fashionable with more highly coloured materials and fuller dresses. Wealthier men and women wore sandals woven from papyrus.

Linen was the most usual material for clothes, although cotton cloth was also available. The skilled and time-consuming business of spinning threads and then weaving them into cloth was done mostly by women. All articles of clothing were hand-made at home. The process began with spinning out thread and ended with sewing together the finished garment.

LOOKING GOOD

If their illustrations are in any way realistic, the guests at an Egyptian party must have looked stunning. Wealthy men and women wore thick black wigs over their shaved heads, rings and earrings, bands on arms, ankles and wrists, and – most striking – huge collars of glittering gold and precious stones. Gold and silver were expensive, so ordinary people had to make do with copper and bronze. Onyx, garnet and amethyst were popular gem stones found locally in Egypt.

One of the more exotic features of Egyptian pictures is the heavy eye make-up shown on men and women, indicating that Egyptians commonly used such make-up on themselves. It consisted of kohl, a dark liner made from lead and oil. As well as making eyes look bigger, it also protected them from the glare of the sun. Nail paint and colouring for the cheeks and lips were also widely used.

➤ A limestone bust (circa 1340 BCE) of the ancient beauty, Queen Nefertiti, wife of King Akhenaten.

MUM, DAD AND THE KIDS

Egyptian society was based on the family and everyday work revolved around the home. The father was head of the family but women were definitely not second-class citizens. They managed the household and were regarded as equal to men in the law courts. Parents left their possessions to both male and female children. Women rarely did the tough manual work that men did, although they might help their husbands with the farming. A few women had very influential positions: before the New Kingdom women priests served in temples and exceptional queens exercised their royal power.

As far as we know, Egyptians did not have formal marriage ceremonies. A couple simply set up house together and shared responsibilities. The common age for doing this was about thirteen for girls and fifteen for boys. Only male members of the royal family (who were allowed to break all the rules!) had more than one wife. Couples might split up if they failed to have children. When this happened relatives and friends made sure that each was treated fairly.

Children were highly prized. There were all kinds of spells, potions and medicines intended to enable a couple to conceive. Although children seem to have been well cared for, childhood was short.

Young people from ordinary backgrounds would be expected to help around the house or farm as soon as they were able, and by ten they would be thinking of an independent future.

Grave evidence

WHAT DOES IT TELL US?

This painted wooden chest used for storing make-up products belonged to Kha, the Director of Works at Deir-el-Medina, and his wife. Found in their tomb, the artefacts remind us that Egyptians were buried with everyday goods that they believed they would need in the Afterlife. The find also reveals the skills of a range of Egyptian craftworkers, including carpenters, painters, potters and cosmetics manufacturers. As wood was scarce and expensive in Egypt, the box also tells us that Kha was wealthy.

Happy family

The parents on the left of this wall painting (c. 1198-1166 BCE) are surrounded by their children while servants bring food and drink. The picture clearly illustrates the long wigs worn by both men and women, and the hair-styles of children. Most prominent is the 'side-lock of youth', a piece of hair left growing from an otherwise shaven head. Notice that it was considered normal for children to go about naked. Egyptian artists typically exaggerated the smaller size of children and also of servants and less important people.

UPHOLDING MAAT

Egyptian law is rather mysterious because right and wrong were based on *Maat* – the religious idea of balance and harmony. Only in the first millennium BCE was the law formally written down. Before then it seems that any official – the vizier, for instance – could act as judge over someone accused of disrupting *Maat*. The king was the highest judge. Many local cases were heard by councils of more important citizens. Occasionally a deity was asked to give a judgement, although it is not known how they announced their decision.

One of the harshest punishments for upper-class Egyptians was exile – being sent out of the country. Fines, prison and beatings were used for lesser crimes. More serious breaches of *Maat* were punished harshly with mutilation of the criminal's body – cutting out the tongue or severing a hand or ear. The ultimate punishment was death. The lucky ones were simply beheaded or drowned. The less fortunate had a wooden stake rammed through their body or were burned alive. Not only that, but it was assumed that the gods would continue to punish them in the next world for having disturbed the heavenly balance of *Maat* on Earth.

SLAVES

Like all ancient civilizations, the Egyptians had slaves. These were usually prisoners of war or foreigners obtained by trading. A slave was not regarded as a person at all, but as a useful animal – like a mule or cat. Without rights, their owner could do what they wanted with them.

This might give a fairly gloomy picture of life as a slave. In fact, only the slaves who worked in mines were really badly treated. Others might be soldiers or, best of all, household servants. Much depended on their masters and mistresses, but in a kind family it was possible for a slave to live a fairly comfortable life.

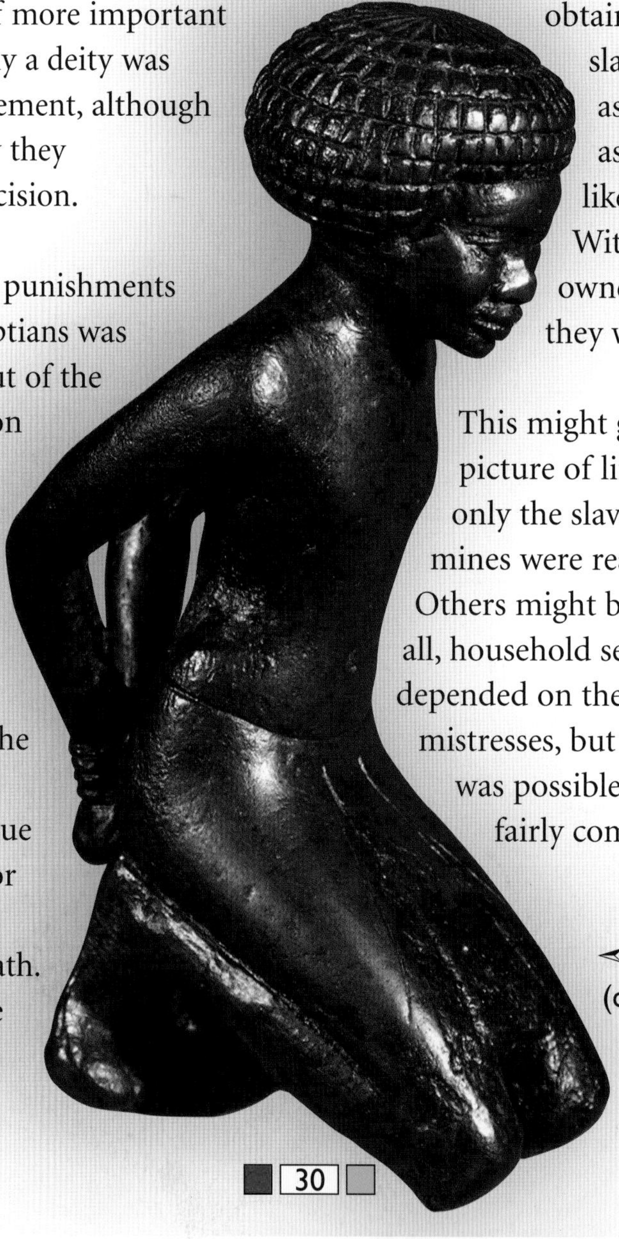

< A bronze figurine (c.1450-1340 BCE) of a slave bound hand and foot.

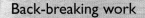

Back-breaking work

WHAT DOES IT TELL US?

In this wall painting of men working in the fields, men sow seed from a basket and hoe with short-handled instruments. This picture tells us something about agriculture in ancient Egypt: the soil deposited by inundation was so light and rich that it did not need to be ploughed before sowing. Instead, it was ploughed or hoed after sowing in order to cover the seeds lying on the surface.

Report of magistrates examining the work of tomb robbers during the reign of Rameses IX:

'The sepulchre of the king, golden sun of the creation, son of the sun, Imhotep … was found to have been broken into. [The thieves] had advanced two and a half cubits [a cubit is the distance from the elbow to the tip of one's fingers]… This is the only damage.'

WHAT DOES IT TELL US?

A thief who tackled a royal shrine risked curses, a terrible death if caught, and certain damnation after death – yet the thieves still went ahead. This would suggest that perhaps not all ancient Egyptians believed in their country's religious system, with the monarch at its head.

HOW DID THE EGYPTIANS COMMUNICATE?

There were two types of education in ancient Egypt, practical and academic. Very few children – less than 1 in 200 – received an academic education. For most Egyptians, 'education' meant learning to do what their parents did.

⋁ An elegantly illustrated Book of the Dead with its hieroglyph writing.

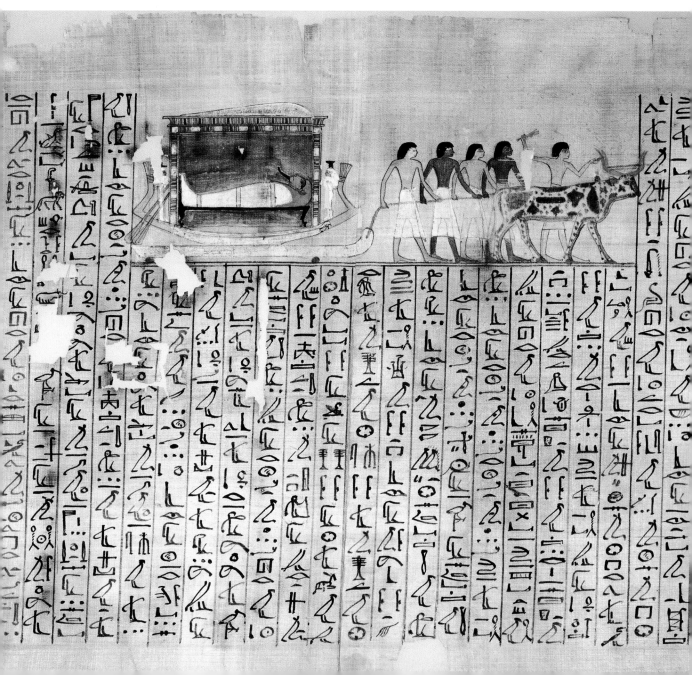

WHAT DOES IT TELL US?

The famous Rosetta Stone is the piece of evidence from which all our understanding of Egyptian writing comes. It was discovered in Rosetta, Egypt, in 1799. The carved text presents the same subject matter in three writing systems: ancient Greek, demotic and hieroglyphic (the latter two forms were used by the ancient Egyptians). In 1822, the brilliant French scholar Jean-Francois Champollion used his knowledge of ancient Greek to become the first person to work out how to decode Egyptian writing.

APPRENTICESHIP

Almost all boys learned their fathers' occupation and skills and continued this work when their fathers died. They became apprenticed to their fathers (or to some other close male relative) at about the age of ten and set about learning on the job. This education usually involved picking up agricultural skills, such as sowing, harvesting and threshing.

During the inundation season (see page 6) farmers went to work on government projects, such as building temples. Their sons went with them and so learned other skills – perhaps brick-making or even carving. Highly skilled craftsmen, such as painters, generally worked at their trade all the year round and did not get involved in farming. Their apprentice sons did the same.

Girls followed much the same pattern as boys, except that they shadowed their mothers in order to learn about work set aside for women. They began their apprenticeship earlier than boys, perhaps starting at the age of eight. The sort of skills they acquired were baby care, cooking, cloth-making and growing fruits and vegetables.

SCHOOLING

Schools, which were only for the upper classes, were attached to important buildings like temples or palaces. As far as we know, only boys had formal schooling, although it is believed that a few aristocratic women also learned to write. We cannot be sure because the examples of women's writing we have may have been dictated by women but written down by men. Many people relied on scribes to write important documents and letters for them.

Driving a royal scribe

WHAT DOES IT TELL US?

This is a carving of the Royal Scribe Ani being driven in his chariot by a slave. One of his titles was 'Accounting Scribe for the Divine Offerings of All the Gods'. His clothing, the personal chariot and the very fact that this image of him was made at all indicate his wealth and importance. It is probably best to think of scribes such as Ani as government officials, rather than just writers.

Lessons were strict, with plenty of corporal punishment, and were often boring. The main way of learning was copying something out many times and memorising it. Boys were taught reading, writing and mathematics. The latter was extremely practical, with no abstract theories. The system was decimal, with signs for one, ten, one hundred and so on up to one million. (The numeral for a million meant 'I can't count this far!') There was no sign for zero. Literacy was taught by scribes, who were among the most important people in Egyptian society. A scribe was not just someone who knew how to read and write. Because they possessed those rare skills they were managers, accountants, officials and organisers. All government business depended on the work of scribes.

WRITING

The first Egyptian writing system developed from pictures. These pictures were simplified into standard shapes, known as hieroglyphs. By the time of the New Kingdom there were about 1,000 of them. There were also signs for ideas and sounds.

A Bas-relief sculpture of two scribes at work (circa 2494-2345 BCE).

Some elements of Egyptian writing were not standardised. The writing could go from left to right, or right to left, top to bottom, or bottom to top, with no punctuation or gaps between words! Not surprisingly, scholars puzzled for centuries to work out what it all meant.

Experts think that hieroglyphic writing was deliberately kept difficult so that only those specially trained could read it. This kept power in the hands of the small minority of educated people. Egyptians also thought symbols could be dangerous: they believed that a picture of something could be as powerful as the thing itself.

Because use of the hieroglyph system was slow and complex, it was usually reserved for formal documents and inscriptions. For everyday writing an easier system was developed – hieratic script. This system had a business form and a literary form. From the business form emerged an even simpler style known as demotic script. Even this was complicated, however, and during Roman times all forms of hieroglyph became obsolete.

Fatherly advice

'Here begins the teaching which the late King of Upper and Lower Egypt … made when he spoke in imparting [giving] truth to his son …'

WHAT DOES IT TELL US?

This is the beginning of a document in which King Amenmessu gives advice to his son. Because there are many documents like this, it seems that such written teachings were designed to be part of an heir's education. They probably had two purposes. First, boys had to write out these teachings, helping with his writing skills. Second, their content passed on the father's wisdom to his son.

WHO DID THE ANCIENT EGYPTIANS WORSHIP?

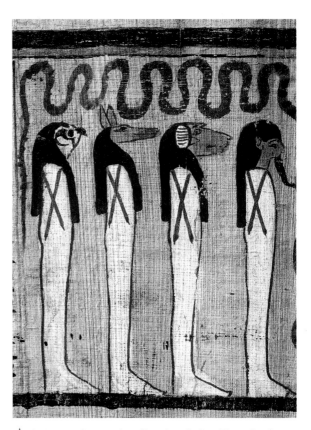

∧ Images from the Book of the Dead of Heruben believed to be of the gods (left to right) Horus, Anubis, Khnum and Ptah.

Ancient Egyptian religion was tremendously important and wickedly complicated! It was important because the king and his subjects believed it was a matter of life or death – not just for individual people but for the whole Earth. It was complicated because, unlike Judaism, Christianity or Islam, it had not been established with a basic set of teachings. Egyptian religion developed over thousands of years and in different parts of the country.

PRESERVING HARMONY

The Egyptians believed everything existed in opposites, such as good/bad, order/chaos, life/death and Egyptians/barbarians. The purpose of religion was to make sure that the good outbalanced the bad; in other words, religion was about warding off chaos (*Isfet*) and maintaining peace, harmony, justice and truth (*Maat*). Doing this required pleasing the gods and goddesses that controlled the world.

Because the Egyptians thought their deities had human and/or animal characteristics, the faithful believed they needed looking after physically rather than just through good words and thoughts (prayer). Tending the gods and goddesses was the purpose of the temples, where they lived. Failure to please a deity, the Egyptians feared, led to punishment. This might be minor, like breaking an arm; but it could also be nation-wide, such as a plague or drought.

Egyptians felt that this system of beliefs explained all that went on in the world.

If foreigners invaded, for instance, the Egyptians believed they were being punished for annoying a powerful deity – perhaps the falcon-god Horus. Because they believed that their religion explained and affected everything, they did not distinguish between religion, magic and science.

CREATION

A good example of the complexity of Egyptian religion is how it explained creation. The beginning of the world has always bewildered human beings, and still does. The Jewish-Christian-Muslim traditions talk of a creator-god, the Garden of Eden and so forth. The Egyptians had three main creation stories, each originating in different parts of the country and at different times.

The creation story from Hermopolis Magna said the first thing to appear was the sun-disk god (Aten), mysteriously made by eight deities of chaos. The Heliopolis story said the sun-god created himself with the aid of magic, then used his bodily fluids to make further new life. A third story was popular at Memphis. It said that the creator-god Ptah made all things by speaking their names. Even more confusing, the Egyptians believed that creation did not happen just once but went on all the time – for example, the sun 'died' every evening and was 'reborn' each morning.

WHAT DOES IT TELL US?

This small gold coffin (c.1347-1337 BCE) held the preserved internal organs of King Tutankhamun and was discovered at Tutankhamun's largely unspoilt tomb in the Valley of the Kings in 1922. The fact that such a beautiful and precious object was made to contain the internal organs of the young king's body shows how important preserving a body was to the ancient Egyptians. This coffin also reflects Tutankhamun's wealth and shows the delightful skills of Egyptian craft workers. Although the king's face may not be realistic, the carving provides information about the royal headdress and false beard, which in real life, was typically tied on with string.

often joined together as the super-deity Amun-Ra. King Akhenaten (1352-1336 BCE) proclaimed the sun-disk god Aten as the supreme and only god, but the idea did not catch on and the Egyptians soon went back to their old multi-deity system.

Three other popular deities were Osiris, Isis and Horus. Osiris was the mummy god of death, birth and rebirth. He and his sister-partner Isis had a son Horus, the falcon-god associated with the kings. A god originally associated with specific places was the crocodile-god Sobek. In time he became so popular that some kings – for example, Sobekneferu (1799-1795 BCE) – added his name to theirs.

One of the leading household gods was Taweret, shown as a female hippopotamus. She had large breasts and sometimes the limbs of a lion and the tail of a crocodile. A kindly deity, Taweret looked after women in childbirth. She

ᴧ A broken sculpture of the head of King Akhenaten.

GODS AND GODDESSES

Two important Egyptian deities were Amun, 'the hidden one', and the sun-god Ra. During the New Kingdom they were

From a Book of the Dead on the Papyrus of Ani (1240 BCE):

'I have not done falsehood [lied] against men, I have not impoverished my associates … I have not deprived the orphan of his property.'

WHAT DOES IT TELL US?

Books of the Dead were buried with a body to help it pass through the Underworld. They consisted of spells and chants to please Osiris, the judge of the dead. The chants quoted above show that, like modern religions, the beliefs of the ancient Egyptians encouraged them to lead good lives on earth so that they might be rewarded in the Afterlife.

this, the priests hoped the deity would
remain contentedly within their temple.

Priests could be full-time or part-time.
They had to keep scrupulously clean and
shave off all bodily hair – even their
eyebrows and eyelashes. Originally some
temples were served by priestesses as well
as priests, but by the New Kingdom priests
had taken over completely. Nevertheless,
women still sang in temple choirs.

Ʌ A relief sculpture of Sobek, the Egyptian
crocodile-god, taken from Kom Ombo
Temple (built during the time of the
Ptolemaic period).

did not have her own temples but was
thought to live in many homes in the
form of a statue or carving on an amulet
(magic charm worn like jewellery).

TEMPLES AND RITUALS

The Egyptians believed that a temple was
often a deity's home. According to their
religion, the spirit of a deity lived in a
statue in the sanctuary at the heart of the
temple. Three times a day priests cleaned
the statue, dressed it in new clothes and
jewellery and left it fresh food. By doing

THE AFTERLIFE

In the ancient Egyptian religion, the death of the earthly body was just a phase of a person's life. People were thought to be able to go on living in a different form after death, and if they did things right their new life might be really enjoyable. This is why bodies were mummified, to preserve them so they could be used in the Afterlife. People were buried with other things they might need, such as their clothes and jewels.

The Egyptians believed that after earthly death, a person entered the long, dark and scary corridors of the Underworld. If they found their way through (helped by a Book of the Dead) they were judged by Osiris. Those who passed the test became holy spirits and lived for ever in happiness. The hearts of those who failed were thrown to the crocodile-lion-hippopotamus 'Swallowing Monster'. When a heart was swallowed, its owner ceased to exist.

Bes the friendly beast

WHAT DOES IT TELL US?

This bronze sculpture is of the household god Bes. He is often shown standing on a lotus flower. The god's ugly face is misleading because he was very popular. His ugliness was probably thought necessary by the Egyptians because he scared snakes away from their houses. The lotus was the flower of Upper Egypt and a symbol of life and rebirth. Its association with Bes reminds us that he was said to help with conception and all areas of human reproduction.

WHAT DOES IT TELL US?

This is a painting of a priest wearing a mask of Anubis, the jackal-headed god of the dead. Anubis was seen as a guardian of places where the dead lay. Why did the Egyptians give the god a jackal head? Probably because jackals were known to dig up and eat dead bodies – it was hoped the jackal-god would stop this from happening. There is another mystery over Anubis: why is he black when real jackals are brown? The answer may be that the god was given the colour of a rotting or mummified body. As a dog-like creature, Anubis also made an ideal guardian of places where the dead lay.

WHAT DID ANCIENT EGYPTIANS CONTRIBUTE TO THE WORLD?

The ancient Egyptians were a proud people. They believed themselves superior to other nations but had little wish to spread their way of life. Nevertheless, other civilizations adopted aspects of Egyptian culture, and some influence our world today.

MEASURING TIME

The Egyptians gave us most of our basic measurements of time. The Egyptian calendar was based upon close observation of the sun, moon and stars. They were the first people to come up with a year of 365 days. Because an actual year is slightly longer (which is why we have leap years), working out ancient Egyptian dates is extremely difficult – especially as their year began in July and dates started afresh with the reign of each new king!

The twenty-four hour day is another Egyptian invention. Egyptians also devised the water-clock to measure the passing of time. Egyptian months were not quite the same as today's. There were twelve in a year, each one was thirty days long. This left five spare days, which they used for religious festivals.

The Abbott Papyrus – an investigation into tomb robberies (circa 1070 BCE):

'Year 15, 19th Athor, was the day when Sha-em-djemi, governor of the town, and Nasiamen, official of the king, scribe of the court, proceeded to the examination of the main sites of the royal family …'

WHAT DOES IT TELL US?

This extract shows us how the Egyptian calendar was used. 'Year 15' is the 15th year of the reign of King Rameses IX. '19th Athor' is the 19th day of the month, which is named after the goddess Athor (normally 'Hathor').

Star-gazing also led them to believe in the power and influence of 'star signs', such as the ones we know as Aries, Taurus and Pisces. These were introduced into Egypt from Babylon in the last millennium BCE. Nowadays, as in ancient Egypt, millions of people still believe their lives are influenced by the heavenly bodies visible in the night sky.

ARCHITECTURE

Until modern times, the most famous Egyptian building design, the pyramid, did not have much impact outside Egypt. The soaring stone columns found in temples and palaces, on the other hand, impacted upon the ancient Greeks in their Doric style of building. This in turn influenced Roman architecture, which featured columns supporting stone beams.

The Greco-Roman (Classical) style of building then fell into disuse before being reintroduced at the time of the Renaissance. Since then it has never really gone out of fashion. Many famous buildings of the modern world, such as the Capitol in Washington DC, USA, show the influence of designs that began in ancient Egypt.

WHAT DOES IT TELL US?

The photograph below shows part of the temple of Amun that King Amenhotep III (c.1390-1352 BCE) built at Luxor. The stone columns, with blocks at the top supporting heavy cross beams, are not so different from the columns found in ancient Greek buildings of the first millennium BCE. We can find this sort of design in some modern buildings, such as the Parthenon in Athens. This suggests the world-wide influence of ancient Egyptian architecture.

WHAT DOES IT TELL US?

According to ancient Egyptian mythology, the soul of a person who has died is weighed against the feather of truth to see whether they have lived an honest life. If the two balance, the person goes to heaven; if the soul is heavier, the person is condemned to hell. This detail of the Judgement of the Dead painting on papyrus illustrates this myth. The idea of judgement preceding heaven or hell appears in later faiths, such as Christianity, and may be part of the religious legacy of ancient Egypt.

MEDICINE

In medicine, as in all other areas of life, the Egyptians did not distinguish between science and religion. Their medicine was what we would call a mixture of reason and magic. However, this did not stop it from being very advanced for its time. Egyptian doctors, especially in Alexandria, were respected by the Greeks, who were among the pioneers of modern scientific medicine.

Scholars believe that by the first millennium BCE some Egyptian doctors had areas of expertise, such as women's medicine. A remarkable document of about 1600 BCE (found in 1862 by Edwin

ʌ Egyptian women making herbal medicine.

Smith, a pioneer in the study of Egyptian science) is a detailed account of ailments and how they should be treated. Some experts say the author of the work, known as the Edwin Smith Medical Papyrus, even understood that blood circulated round the body – some 3,000 years before this was proved scientifically.

Other ancient Egyptian medical documents deal with subjects such as pregnancy and contraception. One Egyptian pregnancy test, using wheat, has been shown to be remarkably accurate. Another medical text prescribes the best medicine for someone bitten by a hippopotamus! Few Egyptian remedies would make much sense to us today, but the attitude behind some of them – that disease, injury and cure can be approached rationally – lies at the heart of modern medicine.

OTHER CONTRIBUTIONS

Because the whole of Egyptian civilization depended upon irrigation of dry land, it pioneered many techniques of moving and preserving water for agriculture. One of the ancient Egyptians' most famous inventions was the *shaduf*. This hand-operated device raised water from a lower to a higher level. The *shaduf* was shaped like a seesaw with a skin or bucket at one end for the water and a counterweight at the other end to raise the bucket. Small *shadufs* can still be seen operating in modern Egypt.

Egyptian art, especially its statues, influenced the work of Greek sculptors. Since the nineteenth century Egyptian artistic styles have been copied in the West, too. Some scholars believe that the popular Egyptian image of Isis and her baby Horus (see below) was the inspiration for Christian pictures and statues of the Virgin Mary and the infant Jesus. The two types of image are often very similar in style and design.

˂ A bronze statue of the goddess Isis and her baby, Horus.

TIMELINE

All dates are BCE and approximate only.

7000-5500	Neolithic Age.
5500-3150	Predynastic Period. Badarians settle in Upper Egypt. Hieroglyphic writing begins.
3150-2690	Archaic Period (Dynasties 1 and 2)
2686-2181	Old Kingdom (Dynasties 3-6) Sphinx and Great Pyramid at Giza built. Wars against Nubians and Libyans.
2181-2055	First Intermediate Period (Dynasties 7-10)
2055-1650	Middle Kingdom (Dynasties 11-14) King Mentuhotep reunites Egypt.
1650-1550	Second Intermediate Period (Dynasties 15-17). Horses introduced. Bronze used.
1550-1069	New Kingdom (Dynasties 18-20). Reigns of Hatshepsut, Thutmose III and Tutankhamun. Tombs built in the Valley of the Kings. Temple of Amenhotep III built at Luxor. Reigns of Rameses II and III.
1069-747	Third Intermediate Period (Dynasties 21-24). Conquest by Nubians.
747-332	Late Period (Dynasties 25-30). Conquest by Assyrians and Persians.
332-305	Conquest by Alexander the Great. Ptolemaic Dynasty.

FURTHER INFORMATION

BOOKS

Stephen Biesty, *Ancient Egypt*, OUP, 2005

Stewart Ross, *Tales of the Dead: Ancient Egypt*, Dorling Kindersley, 2003

T. Deary, *The Awesome Egyptians*, Scholastic, 1997

J. Fletcher, *An Ancient Egyptian Child*, Working White, 1999

J. Shuter, *People Who Made History in Ancient Egypt*, Hodder Wayland, 2001

Jim Pipe, *Pharaoh's Tomb*, Millbrook, 1997

George Hart, *Ancient Egypt*, Dorling Kindersley, 2004

Anthony Allen, *Pharaohs and Pyramids*, Usborne, 2004

WEBSITES

www.ancientegypt.co.uk/menu.html
www.ancient-egypt.org
www.guardians.net/egypt
www.bbc.co.uk/history/ancient/egyptians
www.historyforkids.org/learn/egypt

GLOSSARY

amulet — Magic charm worn by the living or the dead to ward off evil.

archaeology — Studying the past by examining physical remains.

barter — Swap goods rather than buy and sell them for money.

bronze — Metal made by mixing copper and tin.

caravan — Group of merchants travelling together on horse, camel or mule.

chant — Type of religious singing.

civilization — When human beings live in settled communities and farm the land around.

courtier — Person attending the royal court.

deity — God or goddess.

delta — Mouth of a river that spreads into several channels where it enters the sea.

divine — Of a god or goddess.

drought — Time of no rainfall and severe water shortage.

dynasty — Ruling family or time when a single family ruled.

ebony — Hard, dark wood.

empire — Several lands under the rule of an emperor or empress.

export — To trade goods from one country to another.

ferment — Change in a liquid that produces alcohol.

hieroglyph — Ancient Egyptian symbol used as a form of writing.

inscription — Short piece of writing, often carved in stone.

inundation — Flood.

irrigation — Large-scale watering of fields.

kohl — Dark eye-liner.

Intermediate Period — Time when Egypt's government was weak, marked by disorder and sometimes by invasion.

Lower Egypt — Northern Egypt.

Maat — Balance and harmony of all creation.

mummy — Corpse preserved by drying and treating with chemicals.

millennium — 1,000 years.

nomarch — Provincial governor in charge of a nome.

nome — Province.

Nubia — Region of northern Sudan.

papyrus — Tough river reed. The Egyptians made its stems into a type of paper, also called papyrus.

pharaoh — Originally the king's 'great house'. Later, it was used to mean the person from the great house – the king himself.

Renaissance — Movement in arts and culture that occurred in Western Europe from the late 14th century onwards. It is associated with new interest in ancient Greece and Rome.

ritual — Significant religious action done regularly over and over again.

sanctuary — Inner chamber in a church or temple.

scribe — Someone able to read and write.

shrine — Place where a god or goddess is worshipped.

sphinx — Mythical creature with a human head on the body of a lion.

Stone Age — Period of human development before the discovery of metals.

tribute — Payment of money or goods made to please a superior power, such as a king or emperor.

Upper Egypt — Southern Egypt.

vizier — Important minister or adviser.

INDEX